Proclaiming the Passion

The Passion narratives in dramatized form

Church House Publishing

Published by   Church House Publishing
                Church House
                Great Smith Street
                London SW1P 3NZ

Copyright ©   *The Archbishops' Council 2007*

                First published 2007

ISBN   978-0-7151-2126-9

Printed and bound by ArklePrint Ltd, Northampton
Typeset in Gill Sans and Joanna by John Morgan studio
Designed by Derek Birdsall RDI and John Morgan

Contents

1   Introduction

5   Acclamation

6   **Palm Sunday**
        The Passion according to Matthew – *Year A* **6**
        The Passion according to Mark – *Year B* **16**
        The Passion according to Luke – *Year C* **26**

34   **Good Friday**
        The Passion according to John **34**

Introduction

The Passion narratives may be encountered within worship
in a variety of ways: proclaimed by a single voice, read as
a meditation, or presented as a drama. Here the text is set out
for dramatic reading by a number of voices, following a liturgical
custom that has been present in northern Europe since the
tenth century. The dramatic reading of the Passion on Palm
Sunday and Good Friday has become increasingly widespread
throughout the Church of England in recent years, particularly
since the publication of the Passion Narratives in Dramatic
Form in *Lent, Holy Week, Easter* (1986). This edition of the Passion
narratives supplements the liturgical material published
in *Common Worship: Times and Seasons*. The texts printed here are
the Common Worship Lectionary provision for Palm Sunday
and Good Friday. They follow the New Revised Standard Version
(anglicized edition).

Use of the Passion narratives in Holy Week

The accounts of Jesus' Passion are at the heart of the Gospel
tradition; indeed, the four Gospels themselves have often been
described as 'passion narratives with an extended introduction'.
The reading or singing of the Passion narrative is similarly
at the heart of the liturgical celebration of Holy Week. It was
already an important element in the observance of Good Friday
in Jerusalem by the end of the fourth century; by the Middle Ages
in the west, Matthew's Passion was in regular use on Palm Sunday,
and John's on Good Friday, while the others were used during
the intervening days. *The Book of Common Prayer* continued this
tradition, with a few modifications; it fitted well with Cranmer's
concern for the ordered and comprehensive reading of Scripture
in divine service. The use of Matthew's Passion on Palm Sunday
and John's Passion on Good Friday was also retained by the
German Lutheran churches, which is why those two were set
to music by Bach. Common Worship retains the use of John's
Passion on Good Friday, and provides for the other three to be
used on Palm Sunday in successive years.

The four evangelists

The four evangelists tell the same story, but with different
and characteristic emphases. Mark's account is spare and simple:
the true nature of Jesus' messiahship is revealed as he gives
himself in suffering love. Matthew's fuller narrative is concerned
to show how the Scriptures have been literally accomplished
in the details of Jesus' suffering and death. Luke adds unique
details, such as the healing by Jesus of the high priest's servant's
severed ear, or the encounter between Jesus and Herod Antipas.
John shows us a Jesus fully in charge of his own destiny
to the end (19.17). There is no Simon of Cyrene to help carry
his cross, and no cry of final desolation. In John's distinctive
chronology, Jesus dies as the lambs are slain for the celebration
of Passover. When the centurion pierces his side, blood and
water flow from the wound; early Christian commentators
were quick to see them as signs of the sacraments of baptism
and eucharist.

Apportioning the parts

There are many ways in which the Passions may be read.
A traditional custom, deriving from the three sacred ministers
of the High Mass, is for the president to take the part of Jesus,
the deacon the role of the Evangelist, the subdeacon the lesser
individual speaking parts (Peter, Pilate, high priest, centurion
etc.), and the choir or congregation the 'plural' parts (disciples,
priests, soldiers, etc.) and the part of the crowd. This division
works well and may easily be expanded or adapted to fit
the local situation. The parts of Jesus and the Evangelist need
not necessarily be given to liturgical ministers, and the lesser
speaking parts may be distributed among individuals within
the congregation or assigned to a small group of readers.
A distinction might be made between those 'plural' parts that
are sub-sets of the crowd (witnesses, bystanders, passers-by, etc.)
and the others (disciples, priests, soldiers, etc.) that are not.
The former might be taken by small groups distributed
within the congregation and the latter by small groups within
a choir, for example. The congregation's identification with
the crowd in the Matthew and Mark Passions is powerful and
to be encouraged.

Rehearsal

It is vital that the main protagonists (however experienced) are rehearsed in advance of the event. This is especially important in relation to the placing of readers and the use of microphones. All readers need to be clearly audible, and adopt an appropriate pace and style of reading, being able to speak 'in role' without over-acting.

Posture

The dramatic reading of the Passion engages the body, as well as the mind and spirit. It is important, then, that careful thought is given to matters of posture and gesture throughout the reading, in order that everyone present may connect with the reality of the cross. There is a long-established convention of the congregation (except those prevented by infirmity) standing throughout the Passion. There is a sense in which the (slight) discomfort occasioned by this helps us in some small way to identify with the sufferings of Jesus. A traditional custom is to bow or to drop to one knee immediately after the Evangelist has narrated Jesus' death. This simple but profound action can help mark the most solemn and dramatic moment in the text.

Images and music

Where facilities and layout allow, a projected sequence of images can greatly enhance the reading. Images should be carefully selected so as to support the text rather than work against it. As a general rule, they should aim to provide an evocative backdrop to the words, rather than try to be interpretative. Music might also be used as a background to at least some of the reading, though this needs exceptionally careful planning and preparation.

Silence

Silence is an important part of the experience. It is especially appropriate to keep silence after the Evangelist's narration of the death of Jesus. The beginning and ending of the reading are similarly marked by silence. The Evangelist's introduction, 'The Passion of our Lord Jesus Christ according to N', has no congregational response. Likewise, the response to 'This is the Passion of the Lord' is not speech but silence, as we identify ourselves with Jesus in his suffering.

The Passion Narratives

Acclamation

Praise to you, O Christ, King of eternal glory.
Christ humbled himself and became obedient unto death,
even death on a cross.
Therefore God has highly exalted him
and given him the name that is above every name.
Praise to you, O Christ, King of eternal glory.

The Passion according to Matthew
Year A

Voices

Evangelist

Jesus

The following parts may be taken by a third voice

Caiaphas
Centurion
Judas
Peter
Pilate
Pilate's wife
Servant-girl 1
Servant-girl 2

The following parts may be taken by the congregation or choir

Disciples
Priests
Soldiers

Bystanders
Passers-by
Witnesses

Crowd

Matthew 26.14 – 27.66 or Matthew 27.11-54

Evangelist	The Passion of our Lord Jesus Christ according to Matthew.
Evangelist	One of the twelve, who was called Judas Iscariot, went to the chief priests and said,
Judas	What will you give me if I betray him to you?
Evangelist	They paid him thirty pieces of silver. And from that moment he began to look for an opportunity to betray him.
	On the first day of Unleavened Bread the disciples came to Jesus.
Disciples	Where do you want us to make the preparations for you to eat the Passover?
Jesus	Go into the city to a certain man, and say to him, 'The Teacher says, My time is near; I will keep the Passover at your house with my disciples.'
Evangelist	So the disciples did as Jesus had directed them, and they prepared the Passover meal.
	When it was evening, he took his place with the twelve; and while they were eating, he said,
Jesus	Truly I tell you, one of you will betray me.
Evangelist	And they became greatly distressed and began to say to him one after another,
Disciples	Surely not I, Lord?
Jesus	The one who has dipped his hand into the bowl with me will betray me. The Son of Man goes as it is written of him, but woe to that one by whom the Son of Man is betrayed! It would have been better for that one not to have been born.
Evangelist	Judas, who betrayed him, said,
Judas	Surely not I, Rabbi?
Jesus	You have said so.
Evangelist	While they were eating, Jesus took a loaf of bread, and after blessing it he broke it, gave it to the disciples, and said,
Jesus	Take, eat; this is my body.

Evangelist	Then he took a cup, and after giving thanks he gave it to them, saying,
Jesus	Drink from it, all of you; for this is my blood of the covenant, which is poured out for many for the forgiveness of sins. I tell you, I will never again drink of this fruit of the vine until that day when I drink it new with you in my Father's kingdom.
Evangelist	When they had sung the hymn, they went out to the Mount of Olives.
	Then Jesus said to them,
Jesus	You will all become deserters because of me this night; for it is written, 'I will strike the shepherd, and the sheep of the flock will be scattered.' But after I am raised up, I will go ahead of you to Galilee.
Evangelist	Peter said to him,
Peter	Though all become deserters because of you, I will never desert you.
Jesus	Truly I tell you, this very night, before the cock crows, you will deny me three times.
Peter	Even though I must die with you, I will not deny you.
Evangelist	And so said all the disciples.
	Then Jesus went with them to a place called Gethsemane; and he said to his disciples,
Jesus	Sit here while I go over there and pray.
Evangelist	He took with him Peter and the two sons of Zebedee, and began to be grieved and agitated. Then he said to them,
Jesus	I am deeply grieved, even to death; remain here, and stay awake with me.
Evangelist	And going a little farther, he threw himself on the ground and prayed,
Jesus	My Father, if it is possible, let this cup pass from me; yet not what I want but what you want.
Evangelist	Then he came to the disciples and found them sleeping; and he said to Peter,

Jesus	So, could you not stay awake with me one hour? Stay awake and pray that you may not come into the time of trial; the spirit indeed is willing, but the flesh is weak.
Evangelist	Again he went away for the second time and prayed,
Jesus	My Father, if this cannot pass unless I drink it, your will be done.
Evangelist	Again he came and found them sleeping, for their eyes were heavy. So leaving them again, he went away and prayed for the third time, saying the same words. Then he came to the disciples and said to them,
Jesus	Are you still sleeping and taking your rest? See, the hour is at hand, and the Son of Man is betrayed into the hands of sinners. Get up, let us be going. See, my betrayer is at hand.
Evangelist	While he was still speaking, Judas, one of the twelve, arrived; with him was a large crowd with swords and clubs, from the chief priests and the elders of the people. Now the betrayer had given them a sign:
Judas	The one I will kiss is the man; arrest him.
Evangelist	At once he came up to Jesus and said,
Judas	Greetings, Rabbi!
Evangelist	and kissed him.
Jesus	Friend, do what you are here to do.
Evangelist	Then they came and laid hands on Jesus and arrested him. Suddenly, one of those with Jesus put his hand on his sword, drew it, and struck the slave of the high priest, cutting off his ear.
Jesus	Put your sword back into its place; for all who take the sword will perish by the sword. Do you think that I cannot appeal to my Father, and he will at once send me more than twelve legions of angels? But how then would the scriptures be fulfilled, which say it must happen in this way?
Evangelist	At that hour Jesus said to the crowds,
Jesus	Have you come out with swords and clubs to arrest me as though I were a bandit? Day after day I sat in the temple teaching, and you did not arrest me. But all this has taken place, so that the scriptures of the prophets may be fulfilled.

Evangelist	Then all the disciples deserted him and fled.
	Those who had arrested Jesus took him to Caiaphas the high priest, in whose house the scribes and the elders had gathered. But Peter was following him at a distance, as far as the courtyard of the high priest; and going inside, he sat with the guards in order to see how this would end. Now the chief priests and the whole council were looking for false testimony against Jesus so that they might put him to death, but they found none, though many false witnesses came forward. At last two came forward.
Witnesses	This fellow said, 'I am able to destroy the temple of God and to build it in three days.'
Evangelist	The high priest stood up and said,
Caiaphas	Have you no answer? What is it that they testify against you?
Evangelist	But Jesus was silent.
Caiaphas	I put you under oath before the living God, tell us if you are the Messiah, the Son of God.
Jesus	You have said so. But I tell you, from now on you will see the Son of Man seated at the right hand of Power and coming on the clouds of heaven.
Evangelist	Then the high priest tore his clothes and said,
Caiaphas	He has blasphemed! Why do we still need witnesses? You have now heard his blasphemy. What is your verdict?
Priests	He deserves death.
Evangelist	Then they spat in his face and struck him; and some slapped him.
Priests	Prophesy to us, you Messiah! Who is it that struck you?
Evangelist	Now Peter was sitting outside in the courtyard. A servant-girl came to him and said,
Servant-girl I	You also were with Jesus the Galilean.
Evangelist	But he denied it before all of them,
Peter	I do not know what you are talking about.
Evangelist	When he went out to the porch, another servant-girl saw him, and she said to the bystanders,

Servant-girl 2	This man was with Jesus of Nazareth.
Evangelist	Again he denied it with an oath,
Peter	I do not know the man.
Evangelist	After a little while the bystanders came up and said to Peter,
Bystanders	Certainly you are also one of them, for your accent betrays you.
Evangelist	Then he began to curse, and he swore an oath,
Peter	I do not know the man!
Evangelist	At that moment the cock crowed. Then Peter remembered what Jesus had said: 'Before the cock crows, you will deny me three times.' And he went out and wept bitterly. When morning came, all the chief priests and the elders of the people conferred together against Jesus in order to bring about his death. They bound him, led him away, and handed him over to Pilate the governor. When Judas, his betrayer, saw that Jesus was condemned, he repented and brought back the thirty pieces of silver to the chief priests and the elders.
Judas	I have sinned by betraying innocent blood.
Priests	What is that to us? See to it yourself.
Evangelist	Throwing down the pieces of silver in the temple, he departed; and he went and hanged himself. But the chief priests, taking the pieces of silver, said,
Priests	It is not lawful to put them into the treasury, since they are blood money.
Evangelist	After conferring together, they used them to buy the potter's field as a place to bury foreigners. For this reason that field has been called the Field of Blood to this day. Then was fulfilled what had been spoken through the prophet Jeremiah, 'And they took the thirty pieces of silver, the price of the one on whom a price had been set, on whom some of the people of Israel had set a price, and they gave them for the potter's field, as the Lord commanded me.'

The shorter version begins here.

Evangelist	Now Jesus stood before the governor; and the governor asked him,
Pilate	Are you the King of the Jews?
Jesus	You say so.
Evangelist	But when he was accused by the chief priests and elders, he did not answer. Then Pilate said to him,
Pilate	Do you not hear how many accusations they make against you?
Evangelist	But he gave him no answer, not even to a single charge, so that the governor was greatly amazed. Now at the festival the governor was accustomed to release a prisoner for the crowd, anyone whom they wanted. At that time they had a notorious prisoner, called Jesus Barabbas. So after they had gathered, Pilate said to them,
Pilate	Whom do you want me to release for you, Jesus Barabbas or Jesus who is called the Messiah?
Evangelist	For he realized that it was out of jealousy that they had handed him over. While he was sitting on the judgement seat, his wife sent word to him,
Pilate's wife	Have nothing to do with that innocent man, for today I have suffered a great deal because of a dream about him.
Evangelist	Now the chief priests and the elders persuaded the crowds to ask for Barabbas and to have Jesus killed. The governor again said to them,
Pilate	Which of the two do you want me to release for you?
Crowd	Barabbas.
Pilate	Then what should I do with Jesus who is called the Messiah?
Crowd	Let him be crucified!
Pilate	Why, what evil has he done?
Crowd	*(louder)* Let him be crucified!
Evangelist	So when Pilate saw that he could do nothing, but rather that a riot was beginning, he took some water and washed his hands before the crowd.

Pilate	I am innocent of this man's blood; see to it yourselves.
Crowd	His blood be on us and on our children!
Evangelist	So he released Barabbas for them; and after flogging Jesus, he handed him over to be crucified.
	Then the soldiers of the governor took Jesus into the governor's headquarters, and they gathered the whole cohort around him. They stripped him and put a scarlet robe on him, and after twisting some thorns into a crown, they put it on his head. They put a reed in his right hand and knelt before him and mocked him.
Soldiers	Hail, King of the Jews!
Evangelist	They spat on him, and took the reed and struck him on the head. After mocking him, they stripped him of the robe and put his own clothes on him. Then they led him away to crucify him.
	As they went out, they came upon a man from Cyrene named Simon; they compelled this man to carry his cross. And when they came to a place called Golgotha (which means Place of a Skull), they offered him wine to drink, mixed with gall; but when he tasted it, he would not drink it. And when they had crucified him, they divided his clothes among themselves by casting lots; then they sat down there and kept watch over him. Over his head they put the charge against him, which read, 'This is Jesus, the King of the Jews.'
	Then two bandits were crucified with him, one on his right and one on his left. Those who passed by derided him, shaking their heads.
Passers-by	You who would destroy the temple and build it in three days, save yourself! If you are the Son of God, come down from the cross.
Evangelist	In the same way the chief priests also, along with the scribes and elders, were mocking him.
Priests	He saved others; he cannot save himself. He is the King of Israel; let him come down from the cross now, and we will believe in him. He trusts in God; let God deliver him now, if he wants to; for he said, 'I am God's Son.'

Evangelist	The bandits who were crucified with him also taunted him in the same way.
	From noon on, darkness came over the whole land until three in the afternoon. And about three o'clock Jesus cried with a loud voice,
Jesus	Eli, Eli, lema sabachthani?
Evangelist	That is, 'My God, my God, why have you forsaken me?' When some of the bystanders heard it, they said,
Bystanders	This man is calling for Elijah.
Evangelist	At once one of them ran and got a sponge, filled it with sour wine, put it on a stick, and gave it to him to drink. But the others said,
Bystanders	Wait, let us see whether Elijah will come to save him.
Evangelist	Then Jesus cried again with a loud voice and breathed his last.
	At that moment the curtain of the temple was torn in two, from top to bottom. The earth shook, and the rocks were split. The tombs also were opened, and many bodies of the saints who had fallen asleep were raised. After his resurrection they came out of the tombs and entered the holy city and appeared to many. Now when the centurion and those with him, who were keeping watch over Jesus, saw the earthquake and what took place, they were terrified and said,
Centurion	Truly this man was God's Son!
	The shorter version ends here.
Evangelist	Many women were also there, looking on from a distance; they had followed Jesus from Galilee and had provided for him. Among them were Mary Magdalene, and Mary the mother of James and Joseph, and the mother of the sons of Zebedee.
	When it was evening, there came a rich man from Arimathea, named Joseph, who was also a disciple of Jesus. He went to Pilate and asked for the body of Jesus; then Pilate ordered it to be given to him. So Joseph took the body and wrapped it in a clean linen cloth and laid it in his own new tomb, which he had hewn in the rock. He then rolled a great stone to the door of the tomb and went away. Mary Magdalene and the other Mary were there, sitting opposite the tomb.

The next day, that is, after the day of Preparation, the chief priests and the Pharisees gathered before Pilate and said,

Priests   Sir, we remember what that impostor said while he was still alive, 'After three days I will rise again.' Therefore command that the tomb be made secure until the third day; otherwise his disciples may go and steal him away, and tell the people, 'He has been raised from the dead', and the last deception would be worse than the first.

Pilate   You have a guard of soldiers; go, make it as secure as you can.

Evangelist   So they went with the guard and made the tomb secure by sealing the stone.

Evangelist   This is the Passion of the Lord.

No response is made.

The Passion according to Mark
Year B

Evangelist

Jesus

The following parts may be taken by a third voice

Bystander
Centurion
High priest
Judas
Peter
Pilate
Servant-girl

The following parts may be taken by the congregation or choir

Disciples
Priests
Scribes
Soldiers

Bystanders
Passers-by
Witnesses

Crowd

Mark 14.1 – 15.47 or Mark 15.1-39[40-47]

| Evangelist | The Passion of our Lord Jesus Christ according to Mark. |

Evangelist

It was two days before the Passover and the festival of Unleavened Bread. The chief priests and the scribes were looking for a way to arrest Jesus by stealth and kill him; for they said,

Priests

Not during the festival, or there may be a riot among the people.

Evangelist

While he was at Bethany in the house of Simon the leper, as he sat at the table, a woman came with an alabaster jar of very costly ointment of nard, and she broke open the jar and poured the ointment on his head. But some were there who said to one another in anger,

Disciples

Why was the ointment wasted in this way? For this ointment could have been sold for more than three hundred denarii, and the money given to the poor.

Evangelist

And they scolded her. But Jesus said,

Jesus

Let her alone; why do you trouble her? She has performed a good service for me. For you always have the poor with you, and you can show kindness to them whenever you wish; but you will not always have me. She has done what she could; she has anointed my body beforehand for its burial. Truly I tell you, wherever the good news is proclaimed in the whole world, what she has done will be told in remembrance of her.

Evangelist

Then Judas Iscariot, who was one of the twelve, went to the chief priests in order to betray him to them. When they heard it, they were greatly pleased, and promised to give him money. So he began to look for an opportunity to betray him.

On the first day of Unleavened Bread, when the Passover lamb is sacrificed, his disciples said to him,

Disciples

Where do you want us to go and make the preparations for you to eat the Passover?

Evangelist	So he sent two of his disciples, saying to them,
Jesus	Go into the city, and a man carrying a jar of water will meet you; follow him, and wherever he enters, say to the owner of the house, 'The Teacher asks, Where is my guest room where I may eat the Passover with my disciples?' He will show you a large room upstairs, furnished and ready. Make preparations for us there.
Evangelist	So the disciples set out and went to the city, and found everything as he had told them; and they prepared the Passover meal.
	When it was evening, he came with the twelve. And when they had taken their places and were eating, Jesus said,
Jesus	Truly I tell you, one of you will betray me, one who is eating with me.
Evangelist	They began to be distressed and to say to him one after another,
Disciples	Surely, not I?
Jesus	It is one of the twelve, one who is dipping bread into the bowl with me. For the Son of Man goes as it is written of him, but woe to that one by whom the Son of Man is betrayed! It would have been better for that one not to have been born.
Evangelist	While they were eating, he took a loaf of bread, and after blessing it he broke it, gave it to them, and said,
Jesus	Take; this is my body.
Evangelist	Then he took a cup, and after giving thanks he gave it to them, and all of them drank from it.
Jesus	This is my blood of the covenant, which is poured out for many. Truly I tell you, I will never again drink of the fruit of the vine until that day when I drink it new in the kingdom of God.
Evangelist	When they had sung the hymn, they went out to the Mount of Olives. And Jesus said to them,
Jesus	You will all become deserters; for it is written, 'I will strike the shepherd, and the sheep will be scattered.' But after I am raised up, I will go before you to Galilee.

Evangelist	Peter said to him,
Peter	Even though all become deserters, I will not.
Jesus	Truly I tell you, this day, this very night, before the cock crows twice, you will deny me three times.
Peter	*(vehemently)* Even though I must die with you, I will not deny you.
Evangelist	And all of them said the same.
	They went to a place called Gethsemane; and he said to his disciples,
Jesus	Sit here while I pray.
Evangelist	He took with him Peter and James and John, and began to be distressed and agitated. And he said to them,
Jesus	I am deeply grieved, even to death; remain here, and keep awake.
Evangelist	And going a little farther, he threw himself on the ground and prayed that, if it were possible, the hour might pass from him.
Jesus	Abba, Father, for you all things are possible; remove this cup from me; yet, not what I want, but what you want.
Evangelist	He came and found them sleeping; and he said to Peter,
Jesus	Simon, are you asleep? Could you not keep awake one hour? Keep awake and pray that you may not come into the time of trial; the spirit indeed is willing, but the flesh is weak.
Evangelist	And again he went away and prayed, saying the same words. And once more he came and found them sleeping, for their eyes were very heavy; and they did not know what to say to him. He came a third time and said to them,
Jesus	Are you still sleeping and taking your rest? Enough! The hour has come; the Son of Man is betrayed into the hands of sinners. Get up, let us be going. See, my betrayer is at hand.
Evangelist	Immediately, while he was still speaking, Judas, one of the twelve, arrived; and with him there was a crowd with swords and clubs, from the chief priests, the scribes, and the elders. Now the betrayer had given them a sign:
Judas	The one I will kiss is the man; arrest him and lead him away under guard.

Evangelist	So when he came, he went up to him at once and said,
Judas	Rabbi!
Evangelist	and kissed him. Then they laid hands on him and arrested him. But one of those who stood near drew his sword and struck the slave of the high priest, cutting off his ear. Then Jesus said to them,
Jesus	Have you come out with swords and clubs to arrest me as though I were a bandit? Day after day I was with you in the temple teaching, and you did not arrest me. But let the scriptures be fulfilled.
Evangelist	All of them deserted him and fled.
	A certain young man was following him, wearing nothing but a linen cloth. They caught hold of him, but he left the linen cloth and ran off naked.
	They took Jesus to the high priest; and all the chief priests, the elders, and the scribes were assembled. Peter had followed him at a distance, right into the courtyard of the high priest; and he was sitting with the guards, warming himself at the fire.
	Now the chief priests and the whole council were looking for testimony against Jesus to put him to death; but they found none. For many gave false testimony against him, and their testimony did not agree. Some stood up and gave false testimony against him.
Witnesses	We heard him say, 'I will destroy this temple that is made with hands, and in three days I will build another, not made with hands.'
Evangelist	But even on this point their testimony did not agree. Then the high priest stood up before them and asked Jesus,
High priest	Have you no answer? What is it that they testify against you?
Evangelist	But he was silent and did not answer. Again the high priest asked him,
High priest	Are you the Messiah, the Son of the Blessed One?
Jesus	I am; and you will see the Son of Man seated at the right hand of the Power, and coming with the clouds of heaven.

Evangelist	Then the high priest tore his clothes and said,
High priest	Why do we still need witnesses? You have heard his blasphemy! What is your decision?
Evangelist	All of them condemned him as deserving death. Some began to spit on him, to blindfold him, and to strike him, saying to him,
Scribes	Prophesy!
Evangelist	The guards also took him over and beat him.
	While Peter was below in the courtyard, one of the servant-girls of the high priest came by. When she saw Peter warming himself, she stared at him and said,
Servant-girl	You also were with Jesus, the man from Nazareth.
Evangelist	But he denied it:
Peter	I do not know or understand what you are talking about.
Evangelist	And he went out into the forecourt. Then the cock crowed. And the servant-girl, on seeing him, began again to say to the bystanders,
Servant-girl	This man is one of them.
Evangelist	But again he denied it. Then after a little while the bystanders again said to Peter,
Bystanders	Certainly you are one of them; for you are a Galilean.
Evangelist	But he began to curse, and he swore an oath,
Peter	I do not know this man you are talking about.
Evangelist	At that moment the cock crowed for the second time. Then Peter remembered that Jesus had said to him, 'Before the cock crows twice, you will deny me three times.' And he broke down and wept.
	The shorter version begins here.
Evangelist	As soon as it was morning, the chief priests held a consultation with the elders and scribes and the whole council. They bound Jesus, led him away, and handed him over to Pilate. Pilate asked him,
Pilate	Are you the King of the Jews?
Jesus	You say so.

Evangelist	Then the chief priests accused him of many things. Pilate asked him again,
Pilate	Have you no answer? See how many charges they bring against you.
Evangelist	But Jesus made no further reply, so that Pilate was amazed.
	Now at the festival he used to release a prisoner for them, anyone for whom they asked. Now a man called Barabbas was in prison with the rebels who had committed murder during the insurrection. So the crowd came and began to ask Pilate to do for them according to his custom. Then he answered them,
Pilate	Do you want me to release for you the King of the Jews?
Evangelist	For he realized that it was out of jealousy that the chief priests had handed him over. But the chief priests stirred up the crowd to have him release Barabbas for them instead. Pilate spoke to them again,
Pilate	Then what do you wish me to do with the man you call the King of the Jews?
Crowd	Crucify him!
Pilate	Why, what evil has he done?
Crowd	*(louder)* Crucify him!
Evangelist	So Pilate, wishing to satisfy the crowd, released Barabbas for them; and after flogging Jesus, he handed him over to be crucified.
	Then the soldiers led him into the courtyard of the palace (that is, the governor's headquarters); and they called together the whole cohort. And they clothed him in a purple cloak; and after twisting some thorns into a crown, they put it on him. And they began saluting him,
Soldiers	Hail, King of the Jews!
Evangelist	They struck his head with a reed, spat upon him, and knelt down in homage to him. After mocking him, they stripped him of the purple cloak and put his own clothes on him. Then they led him out to crucify him.
	They compelled a passer-by, who was coming in from the country, to carry his cross; it was Simon of Cyrene, the father of Alexander and Rufus.

Then they brought Jesus to the place called Golgotha (which means the place of a skull). And they offered him wine mixed with myrrh; but he did not take it. And they crucified him, and divided his clothes among them, casting lots to decide what each should take.

It was nine o'clock in the morning when they crucified him. The inscription of the charge against him read, 'The King of the Jews.' And with him they crucified two bandits, one on his right and one on his left. Those who passed by derided him, shaking their heads.

Passers-by Aha! You who would destroy the temple and build it in three days, save yourself, and come down from the cross!

Evangelist In the same way the chief priests, along with the scribes, were also mocking him among themselves.

Priests He saved others; he cannot save himself. Let the Messiah, the King of Israel, come down from the cross now, so that we may see and believe.

Evangelist Those who were crucified with him also taunted him.

When it was noon, darkness came over the whole land until three in the afternoon. At three o'clock Jesus cried out with a loud voice,

Jesus Eloi, Eloi, lema sabachthani?

Evangelist which means, 'My God, my God, why have you forsaken me?' When some of the bystanders heard it, they said,

Bystanders Listen, he is calling for Elijah.

Evangelist And someone ran, filled a sponge with sour wine, put it on a stick, and gave it to him to drink, saying,

Bystander Wait, let us see whether Elijah will come to take him down.

Evangelist Then Jesus gave a loud cry and breathed his last. And the curtain of the temple was torn in two, from top to bottom.

Now when the centurion, who stood facing him, saw that in this way he breathed his last, he said,

Centurion Truly this man was God's Son!

The shorter version may end here.

Evangelist   There were also women looking on from a distance; among
them were Mary Magdalene, and Mary the mother of James
the younger and of Joses, and Salome. These used to follow him
and provided for him when he was in Galilee; and there were
many other women who had come up with him to Jerusalem.

When evening had come, and since it was the day of
Preparation, that is, the day before the sabbath, Joseph of
Arimathea, a respected member of the council, who was also
himself waiting expectantly for the kingdom of God, went
boldly to Pilate and asked for the body of Jesus. Then Pilate
wondered if he were already dead; and summoning the
centurion, he asked him whether he had been dead for some
time. When he learned from the centurion that he was dead,
he granted the body to Joseph. Then Joseph bought a linen
cloth, and taking down the body, wrapped it in the linen cloth,
and laid it in a tomb that had been hewn out of the rock.
He then rolled a stone against the door of the tomb. Mary
Magdalene and Mary the mother of Joses saw where the body
was laid.

Evangelist   This is the Passion of the Lord.

No response is made.

The Passion according to Luke
Year C

Voices

Evangelist

Jesus

The following parts may be taken by a third voice

Bystander 1
Bystander 2
Centurion
Peter
Pilate
Robber 1
Robber 2
Servant-girl

The following parts may be taken by the congregation or choir

Disciples
Men
Priests
Soldiers

Luke 22.14 – 23.56 or Luke 23.1-49

| Evangelist | The Passion of our Lord Jesus Christ according to Luke. |

Evangelist — When the hour came, Jesus took his place at the table, and the apostles with him. He said to them,

Jesus — I have eagerly desired to eat this Passover with you before I suffer; for I tell you, I will not eat it until it is fulfilled in the kingdom of God.

Evangelist — Then he took a cup, and after giving thanks he said,

Jesus — Take this and divide it among yourselves; for I tell you that from now on I will not drink of the fruit of the vine until the kingdom of God comes.

Evangelist — Then he took a loaf of bread, and when he had given thanks, he broke it and gave it to them, saying,

Jesus — This is my body, which is given for you. Do this in remembrance of me.

Evangelist — And he did the same with the cup after supper, saying,

Jesus — This cup that is poured out for you is the new covenant in my blood. But see, the one who betrays me is with me, and his hand is on the table. For the Son of Man is going as it has been determined, but woe to that one by whom he is betrayed!

Evangelist — Then they began to ask one another which one of them it could be who would do this.

A dispute also arose among them as to which one of them was to be regarded as the greatest. But he said to them,

Jesus — The kings of the Gentiles lord it over them; and those in authority over them are called benefactors. But not so with you; rather the greatest among you must become like the youngest, and the leader like one who serves. For who is greater, the one who is at the table or the one who serves? Is it not the one at the table? But I am among you as one who serves.

You are those who have stood by me in my trials; and I confer on you, just as my Father has conferred on me, a kingdom, so that you may eat and drink at my table in my kingdom, and you will sit on thrones judging the twelve tribes of Israel.

V	*Evangelist*	Jesus said to Simon Peter,
S	*Jesus*	Simon, Simon, listen! Satan has demanded to sift all of you like wheat, but I have prayed for you that your own faith may not fail; and you, when once you have turned back, strengthen your brothers.
V	*Peter* replied	Lord, I am ready to go with you to prison and to death!
S	*Jesus* said	I tell you, Peter, the cock will not crow this day, until you have denied three times that you know me.

When I sent you out without a purse, bag, or sandals, did you lack anything?

V	*The Disciples* said	No, not a thing.
S	*Jesus* replied	But now, the one who has a purse must take it, and likewise a bag. And the one who has no sword must sell his cloak and buy one. For I tell you, this scripture must be fulfilled in me, 'And he was counted among the lawless'; and indeed what is written about me is being fulfilled.
V	*The Disciples* said	Lord, look, here are two swords.
S	*Jesus* said	It is enough.
V	*Evangelist*	He came out and went, as was his custom, to the Mount of Olives; and the disciples followed him. When he reached the place, he said to them,
S	*Jesus*	Pray that you may not come into the time of trial.
V	*Evangelist*	Then he withdrew from them about a stone's throw, knelt down, and prayed,
S	*Jesus*	Father, if you are willing, remove this cup from me; yet, not my will but yours be done.
V	*Evangelist*	Then an angel from heaven appeared to him and gave him strength. In his anguish he prayed more earnestly, and his sweat became like great drops of blood falling down on the ground.

When he got up from prayer, he came to the disciples and found them sleeping because of grief, and he said to them,

S	*Jesus*	Why are you sleeping? Get up and pray that you may not come into the time of trial.

Evangelist	While he was still speaking, suddenly a crowd came, and the one called Judas, one of the twelve, was leading them. He approached Jesus to kiss him; but Jesus said to him,
Jesus	Judas, is it with a kiss that you are betraying the Son of Man?
Evangelist	When those who were around him saw what was coming, they asked,
Disciples	Lord, should we strike with the sword?
Evangelist	Then one of them struck the slave of the high priest and cut off his right ear. But Jesus said,
Jesus	No more of this!
Evangelist	And he touched his ear and healed him. Then Jesus said to the chief priests, the officers of the temple police, and the elders who had come for him,
Jesus	Have you come out with swords and clubs as if I were a bandit? When I was with you day after day in the temple, you did not lay hands on me. But this is your hour, and the power of darkness!
Evangelist	Then they seized him and led him away, bringing him into the high priest's house. But Peter was following at a distance. When they had kindled a fire in the middle of the courtyard and sat down together, Peter sat among them. Then a servant-girl, seeing him in the firelight, stared at him and said,
Servant-girl	This man also was with him.
Evangelist	But he denied it:
Peter	Woman, I do not know him.
Evangelist	A little later someone else, on seeing him, said,
Bystander 1	You also are one of them.
Peter	Man, I am not!
Evangelist	Then about an hour later yet another kept insisting,
Bystander 2	Surely this man also was with him; for he is a Galilean.
Peter	Man, I do not know what you are talking about!

Evangelist	At that moment, while he was still speaking, the cock crowed. The Lord turned and looked at Peter. Then Peter remembered the word of the Lord, how he had said to him, 'Before the cock crows today, you will deny me three times.' And he went out and wept bitterly.
	Now the men who were holding Jesus began to mock him and beat him; they also blindfolded him and kept asking him,
Men	Prophesy! Who is it that struck you?
Evangelist	They kept heaping many other insults on him.
	When day came, the assembly of the elders of the people, both chief priests and scribes, gathered together, and they brought him to their council. They said,
Priests	If you are the Messiah, tell us.
Jesus *replied*	If I tell you, you will not believe; and if I question you, you will not answer. But from now on the Son of Man will be seated at the right hand of the power of God.
The Priests *asked*	Are you, then, the Son of God?
Jesus *replied simply:*	You say that I am.
Then the Priests *declared:*	What further testimony do we need? We have heard it ourselves from his own lips!

The shorter version begins here.

Evangelist	Then the assembly rose as a body and brought Jesus before Pilate. They began to accuse him.
Priests	We found this man perverting our nation, forbidding us to pay taxes to the emperor, and saying that he himself is the Messiah, a king.
Pilate *asked*	Are you the king of the Jews?
Jesus *replied*	You say so.
Then Pilate *said* to the priests,	I find no basis for an accusation against this man.
Priests *replied (urgently)* but	He stirs up the people by teaching throughout all Judea, from Galilee where he began even to this place.

| Evangelist | When Pilate heard this, he asked whether the man was a Galilean. And when he learned that he was under Herod's jurisdiction, he sent him off to Herod, who was himself in Jerusalem at that time. When Herod saw Jesus, he was very glad, for he had been wanting to see him for a long time, because he had heard about him and was hoping to see him perform some sign. He questioned him at some length, but Jesus gave him no answer. The chief priests and the scribes stood by, vehemently accusing him. Even Herod with his soldiers treated him with contempt and mocked him; then he put an elegant robe on him, and sent him back to Pilate. That same day Herod and Pilate became friends with each other; before this they had been enemies.

Pilate then called together the chief priests, the leaders, and the people, and said to them, |

| Pilate | You brought me this man as one who was perverting the people; and here I have examined him in your presence and have not found this man guilty of any of your charges against him. Neither has Herod, for he sent him back to us. Indeed, he has done nothing to deserve death. I will therefore have him flogged and release him. |

| Evangelist | Then they all shouted out together, |

| Priests | Away with this fellow! Release Barabbas for us! |

| Evangelist | This was a man who had been put in prison for an insurrection that had taken place in the city, and for murder. Pilate, wanting to release Jesus, addressed them again; but they kept shouting, |

| Priests | Crucify, crucify him! |

| Evangelist | A third time he said to them, |

| Pilate | Why, what evil has he done? I have found in him no ground for the sentence of death; I will therefore have him flogged and then release him. |

| Evangelist | But they kept urgently demanding with loud shouts that he should be crucified; and their voices prevailed. So Pilate gave his verdict that their demand should be granted. He released the man they asked for, the one who had been put in prison for insurrection and murder, and he handed Jesus over as they wished. |

Evangelist	As they led him away, they seized a man, Simon of Cyrene, who was coming from the country, and they laid the cross on him, and made him carry it behind Jesus. A great number of the people followed him, and among them were women who were beating their breasts and wailing for him. But Jesus turned to them and said,
Jesus	Daughters of Jerusalem, do not weep for me, but weep for yourselves and for your children. For the days are surely coming when they will say, 'Blessed are the barren, and the wombs that never bore, and the breasts that never nursed.' Then they will begin to say to the mountains, 'Fall on us'; and to the hills, 'Cover us.' For if they do this when the wood is green, what will happen when it is dry?
Evangelist	Two others also, who were criminals, were led away to be put to death with him. When they came to the place that is called The Skull, they crucified Jesus there with the criminals, one on his right and one on his left. Then Jesus said,
Jesus	Father, forgive them; for they do not know what they are doing.
Evangelist	And they cast lots to divide his clothing. And the people stood by, watching; but the leaders scoffed at him.
Priests	He saved others; let him save himself if he is the Messiah of God, his chosen one!
Evangelist	The soldiers also mocked him, coming up and offering him sour wine.
Soldiers	If you are the King of the Jews, save yourself!
Evangelist	There was also an inscription over him, 'This is the King of the Jews.'
	One of the criminals who were hanged there kept deriding him.
Robber 1	Are you not the Messiah? Save yourself and us!
Evangelist	But the other rebuked him.
Robber 2	Do you not fear God, since you are under the same sentence of condemnation? And we indeed have been condemned justly, for we are getting what we deserve for our deeds, but this man has done nothing wrong. Jesus, remember me when you come into your kingdom.

Jesus	Truly I tell you, today you will be with me in Paradise.	
Evangelist	It was now about noon, and darkness came over the whole land until three in the afternoon, while the sun's light failed; and the curtain of the temple was torn in two. Then Jesus, crying with a loud voice, said,	
Jesus	Father, into your hands I commend my spirit.	
Evangelist	Having said this, he breathed his last.	

When the centurion saw what had taken place, he praised God and said,

Centurion Certainly this man was innocent.

Evangelist And when all the crowds who had gathered there for this spectacle saw what had taken place, they returned home, beating their breasts. But all his acquaintances, including the women who had followed him from Galilee, stood at a distance, watching these things.

The shorter version ends here.

Evangelist Now there was a good and righteous man named Joseph, who, though a member of the council, had not agreed to their plan and action. He came from the Jewish town of Arimathea, and he was waiting expectantly for the kingdom of God. This man went to Pilate and asked for the body of Jesus. Then he took it down, wrapped it in a linen cloth, and laid it in a rock-hewn tomb where no one had ever been laid. It was the day of Preparation, and the sabbath was beginning. The women who had come with him from Galilee followed, and they saw the tomb and how his body was laid. Then they returned, and prepared spices and ointments.

On the sabbath they rested according to the commandment.

Evangelist This is the Passion of the Lord.

No response is made.

The Passion according to John

Voices

Evangelist

Jesus

The following parts may be taken by a third voice

Officer
Peter
Pilate
Slave
Woman

The following parts may be taken by the congregation or choir

Priests
Soldiers

Bystanders

John 18.1 – 19.42 (or, if the account of the burial of Christ is to be read later, the Passion Gospel is John 18.1 – 19.37)

Evangelist	The Passion of our Lord Jesus Christ according to John.
Evangelist	Jesus went out with his disciples across the Kidron valley to a place where there was a garden, which he and his disciples entered. Now Judas, who betrayed him, also knew the place, because Jesus often met there with his disciples. So Judas brought a detachment of soldiers together with police from the chief priests and the Pharisees, and they came there with lanterns and torches and weapons. Then Jesus, knowing all that was to happen to him, came forward and asked them,
Jesus	For whom are you looking?
Soldiers	Jesus of Nazareth.
Jesus	I am he.
Evangelist	Judas, who betrayed him, was standing with them. When Jesus said to them, 'I am he', they stepped back and fell to the ground. Again he asked them,
Jesus	For whom are you looking?
Soldiers	Jesus of Nazareth.
Jesus	I told you that I am he. So if you are looking for me, let these men go.
Evangelist	This was to fulfil the word that he had spoken, 'I did not lose a single one of those whom you gave me.' Then Simon Peter, who had a sword, drew it, struck the high priest's slave, and cut off his right ear. The slave's name was Malchus. Jesus said to Peter,
Jesus	Put your sword back into its sheath. Am I not to drink the cup that the Father has given me?
Evangelist	So the soldiers, their officer, and the Jewish police arrested Jesus and bound him. First they took him to Annas, who was the father-in-law of Caiaphas, the high priest that year. Caiaphas was the one who had advised the Jews that it was better to have one person die for the people.

Evangelist	Simon Peter and another disciple followed Jesus. Since that disciple was known to the high priest, he went with Jesus into the courtyard of the high priest, but Peter was standing outside at the gate. So the other disciple, who was known to the high priest, went out, spoke to the woman who guarded the gate, and brought Peter in. The woman said to Peter,
Woman	You are not also one of this man's disciples, are you?
Peter	I am not.
Evangelist	Now the slaves and the police had made a charcoal fire because it was cold, and they were standing round it and warming themselves. Peter also was standing with them and warming himself.
	Then the high priest questioned Jesus about his disciples and about his teaching. Jesus answered,
Jesus	I have spoken openly to the world; I have always taught in synagogues and in the temple, where all the Jews come together. I have said nothing in secret. Why do you ask me? Ask those who heard what I said to them; they know what I said.
Evangelist	When he had said this, one of the police standing nearby struck Jesus on the face, saying,
Officer	Is that how you answer the high priest?
Jesus	If I have spoken wrongly, testify to the wrong. But if I have spoken rightly, why do you strike me?
Evangelist	Then Annas sent him bound to Caiaphas the high priest.
	Now Simon Peter was standing and warming himself. They asked him,
Bystanders	You are not also one of his disciples, are you?
Peter	I am not.
Evangelist	One of the slaves of the high priest, a relative of the man whose ear Peter had cut off, asked,
Slave	Did I not see you in the garden with him?
Evangelist	Again Peter denied it, and at that moment the cock crowed.

Then they took Jesus from Caiaphas to Pilate's headquarters. It was early in the morning. They themselves did not enter the headquarters, so as to avoid ritual defilement and to be able to eat the Passover. So Pilate went out to them and said,

Pilate   What accusation do you bring against this man?

Priests   If this man were not a criminal, we would not have handed him over to you.

Pilate   Take him yourselves and judge him according to your law.

Priests   We are not permitted to put anyone to death.

Evangelist   This was to fulfil what Jesus had said when he indicated the kind of death he was to die.

Then Pilate entered the headquarters again, summoned Jesus, and asked him,

Pilate   Are you the King of the Jews?

Jesus   Do you ask this on your own, or did others tell you about me?

Pilate   I am not a Jew, am I? Your own nation and the chief priests have handed you over to me. What have you done?

Jesus   My kingdom is not from this world. If my kingdom were from this world, my followers would be fighting to keep me from being handed over to the Jews. But as it is, my kingdom is not from here.

Pilate   So you are a king?

Jesus   You say that I am a king. For this I was born, and for this I came into the world, to testify to the truth. Everyone who belongs to the truth listens to my voice.

Pilate   What is truth?

Evangelist   After he had said this, he went out to the Jews again and told them,

Pilate   I find no case against him. But you have a custom that I release someone for you at the Passover. Do you want me to release for you the King of the Jews?

Priests   Not this man, but Barabbas!

Evangelist   Now Barabbas was a bandit.

Evangelist	Then Pilate took Jesus and had him flogged. And the soldiers wove a crown of thorns and put it on his head, and they dressed him in a purple robe. They kept coming up to him, saying,
Soldiers	Hail, King of the Jews!
Evangelist	and striking him on the face. Pilate went out again and said to them,
Pilate	Look, I am bringing him out to you to let you know that I find no case against him.
Evangelist	So Jesus came out, wearing the crown of thorns and the purple robe.
Pilate	Here is the man!
Evangelist	When the chief priests and the police saw him, they shouted,
Priests	Crucify him! Crucify him!
Pilate	Take him yourselves and crucify him; I find no case against him.
Priests	We have a law, and according to that law he ought to die because he has claimed to be the Son of God.
Evangelist	Now when Pilate heard this, he was more afraid than ever. He entered his headquarters again and asked Jesus,
Pilate	Where are you from?
Evangelist	But Jesus gave him no answer.
Pilate	Do you refuse to speak to me? Do you not know that I have power to release you, and power to crucify you?
Jesus	You would have no power over me unless it had been given you from above; therefore the one who handed me over to you is guilty of a greater sin.
Evangelist	From then on Pilate tried to release him, but the Jews cried out,
Priests	If you release this man, you are no friend of the emperor. Everyone who claims to be a king sets himself against the emperor.
Evangelist	When Pilate heard these words, he brought Jesus outside and sat on the judge's bench at a place called The Stone Pavement, or in Hebrew Gabbatha. Now it was the day of Preparation for the Passover; and it was about noon. He said to the Jews,

Pilate	Here is your King!
Priests	Away with him! Away with him! Crucify him!
Pilate	Shall I crucify your King?
Priests	We have no king but the emperor.
Evangelist	Then he handed him over to them to be crucified.
	So they took Jesus; and carrying the cross by himself, he went out to what is called The Place of the Skull, which in Hebrew is called Golgotha. There they crucified him, and with him two others, one on either side, with Jesus between them. Pilate also had an inscription written and put on the cross. It read, 'Jesus of Nazareth, the King of the Jews.' Many of the Jews read this inscription, because the place where Jesus was crucified was near the city; and it was written in Hebrew, in Latin, and in Greek. Then the chief priests of the Jews said to Pilate,
Priests	Do not write, 'The King of the Jews', but, 'This man said, I am King of the Jews.'
Pilate	What I have written I have written.
Evangelist	When the soldiers had crucified Jesus, they took his clothes and divided them into four parts, one for each soldier. They also took his tunic; now the tunic was seamless, woven in one piece from the top. So they said to one another,
Soldiers	Let us not tear it, but cast lots for it to see who will get it.
Evangelist	This was to fulfil what the scripture says, 'They divided my clothes among themselves, and for my clothing they cast lots.' And that is what the soldiers did.
	Meanwhile, standing near the cross of Jesus were his mother, and his mother's sister, Mary the wife of Clopas, and Mary Magdalene. When Jesus saw his mother and the disciple whom he loved standing beside her, he said to his mother,
Jesus	Woman, here is your son.
Evangelist	Then he said to the disciple,
Jesus	Here is your mother.
Evangelist	And from that hour the disciple took her into his own home.

Evangelist	After this, when Jesus knew that all was now finished, he said (in order to fulfil the scripture),
Jesus	I am thirsty.
Evangelist	A jar full of sour wine was standing there. So they put a sponge full of the wine on a branch of hyssop and held it to his mouth. When Jesus had received the wine, he said,
Jesus	It is finished.
Evangelist	Then he bowed his head and gave up his spirit.

Since it was the day of Preparation, the Jews did not want the bodies left on the cross during the sabbath, especially because that sabbath was a day of great solemnity. So they asked Pilate to have the legs of the crucified men broken and the bodies removed. Then the soldiers came and broke the legs of the first and of the other who had been crucified with him. But when they came to Jesus and saw that he was already dead, they did not break his legs. Instead, one of the soldiers pierced his side with a spear, and at once blood and water came out. (He who saw this has testified so that you also may believe. His testimony is true, and he knows that he tells the truth.) These things occurred so that the scripture might be fulfilled, 'None of his bones shall be broken.' And again another passage of scripture says, 'They will look on the one whom they have pierced.'

If the account of the burial of Christ is to be read later, the Passion Gospel ends here.

Evangelist	After these things, Joseph of Arimathea, who was a disciple of Jesus, though a secret one because of his fear of the Jews, asked Pilate to let him take away the body of Jesus. Pilate gave him permission; so he came and removed his body. Nicodemus, who had at first come to Jesus by night, also came, bringing a mixture of myrrh and aloes, weighing about a hundred pounds. They took the body of Jesus and wrapped it with the spices in linen cloths, according to the burial custom of the Jews. Now there was a garden in the place where he was crucified, and in the garden there was a new tomb in which no one had ever been laid. And so, because it was the Jewish day of Preparation, and the tomb was nearby, they laid Jesus there.

Evangelist   This is the Passion of the Lord.

　　　　　　　No response is made.